Women Winning at Work

WOMEN WINNING AT WORK

A 21-DAY GUIDE TO EXPERIENCING SPIRITUAL SUCCESS IN THE FACE OF WORKPLACE DIFFICULTY

Tiffany A. Washington

Cover Photo:
Point and Click Photography
www.pointandclick-photography.com

Editor:
Shannan E. Johnson
The Professional Pen
www.awriterforyourwriter.com

Titles by Tiffany A. Washington may be purchased in bulk for educational, business or promotional use. This includes, but is not limited to, book clubs and bible study groups.

Transformation7 by Tiffany A. Washington
www.transformation7.com
www.facebook.com/T7byTiffany
www.womenwinningatwork.com

ISBN: 0998696706
ISBN 13: 9780998696706

This devotional is a testament of God's love for us, even through tumultuous times at work.
Trust Him.

ACKNOWLEDGEMENTS

To my mother, who has served as my earthly rock and sounding board. You have trained me up in the way I should go and taught me the power of prayer. I am so thankful that I don't have to scale the mountains alone, for you are always by my side. I love you.

Contents

	Author's Note	xv
	There is Purpose in the Process: Conquering Worklife Woes	xvii
Section I Part I	**Acknowledge the Challenge**	1
	When you are Worried	3
	When you are Under Attack	7
	Colliding with Naysayers	11
	When you feel Defeated	15
Section I Part II	**Seek God**	19
	Perfectly Imperfect	21
	Feeling Undervalued and Unappreciated	25

	Getting Unstuck	29
	Finding Hope through Hurt	33
Section I Part III	**Find Peace through Him**	37
	I am not Alone	39
	Finding Peace	43
	Walking in the Light of God	47
	God Is Where the Good Stuff Is	51
Section I Part IV	**Change your Perspective**	55
	From Fear to Faith	57
	Turning the Other Cheek	61
	Pray your Way	65
	Practicing the Fruits	71
Section I Part V	**Enjoy the Journey**	75
	Being Productive	77
	Walking it Out	81
	Enjoying the Journey	85
	Promoting Positivity	89

	Spirit of Thanksgiving	93
	You Made It!	97
Section II Part I	**Reflection Section**	99
Section II Part II	**Work Hag Worry**	123
	How to Use this Section	125
	Biblical References	149
	About the Author A Touch of Tiffany	159
	How to Contact Tiffany A. Washington	163

AUTHOR'S NOTE

Sometimes, work just sucks. Getting out of the bed each morning to carry on a routine day after day with little change in you or the people around you can be a bit underwhelming and uninspiring. Further, when carrying out the duties of your daily vocation, it does not help that you may have to engage with people who mean you harm and seemingly do everything in their power to make your worklife uncomfortable or even miserable. Some even go as far as dehumanizing and devaluing your worth as a human being. I call these human annoyances *work hags* – maliciously vicious colleagues whose primary goal is to void the workplace of positive human interaction and use their venomous nature to poison the climate and culture of work communities.

Over the course of time, you will encounter several workplace characters and circumstances that force you to experience inexplicable emotions that you never intended to grapple with while at work. Beware! This will include the infamous work hag. The awesome thing is that each circumstance you face will propel you into a positive place of growth if you allow God to transform those moments of unproductivity, pain, frustration, fear and sadness into fruitful, joy-filled moments wrapped with patience, love, and enlightenment.

Through this book, your thinking about workplace challenges will be confronted with poignant scripture, thoughtful commentary, and powerful prayer that will help you to address all of the workplace scenarios typical to most careers. When facing hardships at work, it is important to combat the negative with the power of God's word. This is a 21-day devotional dedicated to people who wish to infuse their lives with prayer that battles everyday demons.

There is Purpose in the Process: Conquering Worklife Woes

As a participant in the workforce daily grind, I have faced painful moments in my life that challenged the way I think about and approach work and my relationships with coworkers. These shifts in thought and behaviors have required my total reliance and dependence on God. Repeated brutal interactions shredded my self-esteem and left me feeling like I was inadequate at fulfilling the responsibilities of my job. Though my memories are imperfect, I would like to share a bit of my worklife journey with you.

A Real-Life Work Hag

Much of my adult experience in the workplace has centered on relationships with other women, and over the course of my work years, I prided myself on getting along with others. Unfortunately, while serving in the educational sector as an assistant principal, I encountered a relationship of threatening and demeaning snubs that were blatant attempts to sully my name and the career that I was building. Needless to say, the ultimate work hag was bullying me.

Throughout the 2013 Fall Semester, my work hag continually harassed me. I vividly remember her needing to speak with me one day. Our offices were on two different floors, so she called my extension saying she needed to talk to me. I told her that I was conferencing with a teacher and would get back with her after the conclusion of my meeting. No less than five minutes later, she called my extension again. Because she had not stated the urgency of her needs, I ignored the call and continued meeting with my teacher.

The phone rang again…and again…and again…totaling eleven times. The teacher with whom I was conferencing looked confused, but she refrained from asking questions. Shortly after the last set of rings, we heard footsteps coming closer to my open door. A shadow cast the floor preceding the presence of my work hag. Did she really just interrupt my meeting?

In disbelief, I said, "Yes," acknowledging her presence.

She said, "The books need to be labeled for the department."

Knowing that this comment could have waited, I stood up, looked at her for a moment befuddled by her need to bark orders at me, and calmly said, "Okay. I'm in a meeting, so it will have to wait."

She turned and walked away, huffing and mumbling under her breath as if I had done something to annoy her. I refocused my attention on the teacher and completed the meeting. Though neither of us mentioned the awkward moment, we were both equally disturbed.

Incidents such as the aforementioned happened consistently – from being yelled at in the hallway for not lining up students the exact way that she wanted to being ignored when I tried to get her attention. She belittled my authority in front of adults and attempted to discredit me in front of my principal by saying things like, "You should know this," and "I don't know why you are over this department anyway." She craved blood and she wasn't satisfied until it was drawn.

Her behavioral antics forced an equally ranked administrator and a teacher to resign within weeks of the 2013-2014 school year, but I was determined to walk through the storm as my mother had coached me. Although I wasn't the only one subjected to her wrath, she seemed to enjoy my pain the most. She feasted on my meekness and became more engorged with each bow of my head. She washed it all down with the tears that formed small puddles in the corners of my eyes. Daily, I subjected myself to this woman's tempest nature because I needed my job. In the midst of it all, I learned that I had allowed my day to be good or bad based on my interactions with the work hag.

I attempted to resolve the unknown conflict peacefully: first with her alone, then with a mediator, and finally with our assigned mentor and the campus principal—all to no avail. This young woman with whom I had multiple traumatic encounters never revealed why she took issue with me. She just resorted to being a 'mean girl' without a cause. I wondered how someone could be so intentionally cruel. Her need for attention swept me into in a whirlwind of severe disappointment and unproductivity that swelled into staying in the bed until the very last minute because I feared going to work and failing to contain my excessive crying. My angst led to a decreased appetite; consequently, I lost 20 pounds. I sought out a mental health professional because I had never had any bouts with "feeling low" in the past. I learned that I was experiencing situational depression and realized that my health was at risk.

While walking through this worklife storm, I was simply going through the motions: wake up, coach myself out of the bed, report to work, get harassed, take my verbal beating, cry about it, go home, get directly in the bed – start over the next day. I allowed myself to become weak misconstruing my passiveness for professionalism. Because I could not afford to leave my job, I knew I had to continue going to work and battle daily for my own sanity. I wanted to quit and just go to a place where I did not have to worry about climbing the corporate ladder of success or being accountable for anyone but myself. I came to crave little involvement with others. My work hag had made this once bold, assertive and creative person a timid soul who cowered in corners hiding from public shame and humiliation.

At the helm of this work hag experience, no resolution had been found. It was then that I knew that I was fighting with spirits that could only be cast out through prayer. Going through this stage of life brought back memories of watching my mother pray daily at home and every Sunday in the pulpit. Through her bold prayers in the midst of various struggles, she spoke what seemed to be out of reach into existence. She taught me how to walk through the storm by uttering my specific requests to God. So, just like mama, I prayed for my breakthrough and started a new prayer ritual, "God, deliver me." I prayed that plea every morning and studied spiritual warfare every night before bed. In order to fight my best fight, I wanted to be familiar with the spirit I was carrying (spirit of fear), and the spirit of my work hag (spirit of haughtiness/pride).

After much contemplation and prayer, I decided that I wasn't going to be able to sustain sanity in my place of work, and I finally reported each incident of workplace bullying to the highest local in-district authority, the school supervisor. She came to my campus unexpectedly in response to my complaint. Feeling unprepared and prematurely defeated, I made my way to her designated office after scrambling to get my notes together so that I could easily reference all of the negative occurrences from the work hag. Now sitting across from the school supervisor, I silently wept as I explained the incidents. Unfortunately, there is no crying in the field of education. You suck it up and move on. But I could not.

There is no way someone should be able to mistreat others and have no consequences.

The school supervisor listened and debated with me a bit, calling some of my accounts non-consequential. She asked me what I wanted, and I told her that I would like to transfer to a different school. The answer was…no. There were no vacancies in her jurisdiction. My options were to stay at my current campus or resign. I knew the latter wasn't a tangible option. I had to support myself, so I accepted the no and continued showing up every day to even more verbal abuse and hard stares from the work hag because my report to the school supervisor infuriated her. Yet, I don't think she even got a slap on the wrist for her outlandish behavior.

After enduring a semester of my dedicated work hag, I went home for Christmas break concerned about my next move. I was consumed with the thought of what would happen once I returned to school. I knew that I could not survive another semester of the torment, so I began to pray like I had never prayed before. I prayed when I woke up, prayed while I was watching television and I even prayed while I exercised. Once the new year came, I was feeling stronger. Prayer led me to confidently weather the storm. Even if a tornado came close to me, I was determined to not get caught in the funnel.

On the first day back to school, I walked in with my head held high and my high heels on (I had totally stopped wearing my beloved shoes once I got into the thick of things during the previous semester). The first week of school passed with very little interaction from my work hag (Thank you, Jesus! She was leaving me alone.). By the time the second week rolled around, the school supervisor called me into my principal's office about a spot becoming available; I had been granted a transfer. I asked her when and she simply stated, "Tomorrow." Won't the Lord do it! My spirit leapt for joy. I did not care where the new assignment was, I just wanted to get away from the demon that plagued my soul.

God delivered me from a dire situation, one that nearly took me out. The experience taught me that sometimes you just have to walk through the storm. You may get bruised, your clothes may become a bit tattered, and your hair may become disheveled, but there is always a message in the mess. My wounds healed and I learned how to make it through tough circumstances by leaning on the strength of the Lord. Through his deliverance, I was better able to handle the next set of work hags. Though they didn't prove to be as rough as my first hag, they actually solidified my decision to write this book. I praise God for allowing my experiences to mold the words set before you!

Dazed and Confused

Now 2015, I was completing my second year as an assistant principal with minimal disruption, and it was time to attain exactly what I had been training for – becoming a principal. After spending a full year and a half at the school where I transferred, I successfully made it into the districts' principal applicant pool. What an honor to say that my two-year master's program had prepared me for this glorious moment in my career. I had all the formal educational leadership training prior to encountering my work hag, and the district had even paid for me to participate in the prestigious program where I earned my advanced degree. It was now March, the month when principal vacancies were scouted, and I would certainly not have any problems obtaining a coveted principal position. I did good work, produced results, and my reputation was untarnished, or so I thought.

Three months of silence passed. I could not get an interview to save my life! Something had to be wrong with the system. How could the district pay for my graduate-level education and NOT hire me to lead a school? Why make an investment that you don't cash-in? The phone was not ringing, the email was not dinging, and no one was there to guide me through the process of getting in front of district hiring managers.

I wracked my brain over the silence. I've never worked hard and not gotten what I wanted (I know. Spoiled right?). I applied and applied and applied some more. Finally, I got one interview just as July was coming to a close; I wasn't selected. Though having face time with a hiring manager was important, being overlooked made disappointment overtake me once more.

My summer was spent in solitude wondering why the Lord had brought me through so much mess and didn't reward me with what I wanted! I later found out that my previous school supervisor shared with hiring managers that I was not "strong enough" to lead a school based on her account of my experience with workplace bullying. But, I refused to be stigmatized based on one person's version of the truth. I decided that playing small was no longer an option for me. Being passed over for opportunities to interview because one person's perception of me placed me in a bucket labeled 'do not touch' was unacceptable. I licked my wounds and morphed into what is standardly known as 'male behavior.' I quickly learned how to let every distraction roll off my back like a duck out of water. I walked with confidence, smiled when I wanted to cry and opted to spit knowledge in response to ignorance rather than respond in kindness.

During this time of faux posturing, I realized that I was still dealing with the remnants of the work hag. Crying is unacceptable in education, and because of my reaction to my work hag, I was not being hired as a principal. Too many tears equal weakness, something that can't be shown when leading others. Though I understood that, I also knew that I was highly qualified for the position. I could not let my distress win if I was going to prove my leadership skills.

My 21-Day Journey

With the new 2015-2016 school year looming, I prayed to the Lord for His guidance and clarity regarding next steps for my career. Crying out to him, "Lord, help," was all I could utter on some days, unable to muster the energy for much else. Two weeks after school began, a very close friend of mine invited me to participate in the Daniel Fast, a 21-day retreat from certain foods as a sign of sacrifice to the Lord. Seeing the clouds of gloom creeping into my life, I knew that making this bold sacrifice to God would let Him know how serious I was about changing my life. So, I jumped at the opportunity to fast with a group of like-minded women. The built-in support was just what I needed in order to tackle the 21-day journey.

My specific focus over the course of the fast was to gain clarity about my career path. When I entered the fast, I was still brooding with devastation. "Lord, what would you have me to do?" I am unhappy, immobilized, and drained. I didn't need to be belittled, micromanaged, or stifled at the hands of someone else. A new question emerged: "Should I quit my job, Lord?" Each day I prayed for an answer and sought Him through scripture, but it seemed like the more I prayed, the tougher things got at work. My supervisor was riding me HARD. She expressed to me that she could sense a change in my demeanor that was causing a withdrawal from my day-to-day work process. I wasn't contributing as much, speaking up as much or being as much of a 'go-getter.' Sadly, she was right. I had relegated myself into a corner, cowering in my own defeat. Disengaged, I came to work as a duty, or better yet, an obligation to my paycheck.

After our conversation, I pouted and, for a moment, reverted to my selfish, spoiled only-child behavior. My daily interaction with colleagues was just shy of a disgruntled toddler who sucks her finger as she holds on to her stuffed animal for comfort. Though I knew this was no way to behave, I gave in to the fleshly desire to throw myself a pity-party. Anyone who was interested in joining me in the rain could definitely get their rain boots and trudge with me through the mud.

While praying over the 21 days, I asked God for a better attitude in the midst of walking through the pain of rejection. I claimed that prayer would boost my personal morale and help me to be more effective on the job. I couldn't let my defeat stagnate my career. It would not continue to have that kind of power over my life.

As the fast progressed, the weight of my disappointment started to lift. Praying diligently each day provided clarity and peace. Who was I to sulk and feel sorry because the world did not revolve around me? God made me to be a bright light that overcomes darkness, not a flickering candle that can easily be blown out by the wind. Fed up with my own frustration, I slowly made the choice to ascend my anger and devote myself to working smarter. I began smiling and tackling projects with renewed energy. Work kept piling up, but I developed processes to be more efficient and committed to staying the course until it was all done. God was restoring both my cheerful attitude and my broken heart. I accepted the healing without resistance.

On the 22nd day, the day after the Daniel Fast had ended, the women scheduled a virtual meetup in our private group where we all shared our breakthroughs. Overjoyed, I reported that I was quitting my job! Burned out in my current role, I knew that a lateral move to a different campus would not be fulfilling, and I knew that I would not pursue a principalship again. While fasting, God revealed to me that it was time to transition to the next phase of my journey. The restored gift of my upbeat attitude allowed me to see brighter glimpses of my life. I saw flickers of my future, though not completely clear, that included spending more time writing and speaking, two divine gifts placed within me at an early age that I used regularly in my educational career to professionally develop and train teachers. I executed these gifts with excellence in my career, but it was time for me to use my talents in a different manner. Though I was met with slight hesitation, the close friends with whom I shared my exciting news embraced the thought of me starting a new chapter.

The next leg of this life tour would be something much different than my current role. God had yet to completely reveal my next steps, but I knew it would be something great. I have always wanted to motivate and inspire others on a larger scale. Since childhood, I knew that I wanted to be a motivational speaker and writer. I cut my oratorical and writing teeth growing up in church, developing the skills more through school and my professional career. I regularly performed original poems and wrote plays for my students' performances. As my talent progressed, I picked up freelance work as a ghostwriter, which further tickled my ambition to incorporate writing into my future. Because of my past involvement with speaking and writing, I had an inkling that God would draw me closer to my original love.

Through the fast, God confirmed that my earthly rejection by people was not His denial. It was actually my sanctified promotion! No longer would I have to pour every ounce of myself into a thankless job while sitting under the guise of others who did not mean well. No longer would I have to build someone else's dream while stifling my own. If I could work this hard for someone else, surely I could work as hard for myself, perhaps in a business that uses my writing and speaking skills to inform women of how to handle each other through the eyes of patience, understanding, and, most importantly, love. God allowed me to see glimpses of these initial business triggers, leading me to my decision to let go and let God.

This clarity made the wind finally start to blow in my direction. I felt a cool breeze each time I reported to work. My energy revved up, and I was back to my old self doing everything with excellence and holding both my team and myself to the highest standards of performance. Not even the 100-degree, southern weather could kill my positive vibe. My drought was about to be over, and I would soon walk out of the desert into a land abounding with grace and opportunity. Because I knew that I was laboring towards my next destination, there was very little that could ruffle my feathers. I worked the Daniel Fast, and through the fast, God worked on me!

The Second-Time Around

Since the Daniel Fast was such an amazing experience, I decided to do it again, without invitation, in January 2016. I woke up every morning at 4:00am, an hour and a half before my usual alarm, to write about the different emotions I felt over the course of my career. I pondered about how to help women with their daily work struggles. For three years, the feelings of angst, doubt, and frustration kept resurfacing in my professional life; certainly, I was not the only one. What did other women like me need in order to get over the hurdles faced at work? What tools and resources could I have used while I was battling situational depression, workplace bullying, and unproductivity? I wrote about my journey to help women understand that suffering is a choice, not a mandate.

Then it became clear. For this fasting journey, I would achieve becoming a woman of influence through the avenue of writing and I would consider signing up for the district's early resignation program, which includes a small monetary incentive for notifying the district early if you are not returning. On the one hand, applying for the incentive could help me stay afloat while becoming a full-time writer. However, early resignation can have an affect on the work environment that isn't always positive.

I could be met with congratulations on the new leg of my journey leaving my last days filled with support and a pleasant pace of work. On the other hand, my coworkers may project feelings of jealousy and resentment by leaving all the work to pile up on me. Or I could be micromanaged to ensure that I keep up with all of my tasks because it is assumed that I will only do the minimum at work. Interestingly, I was met with all of the above. However, the assumption that I would lose my work ethic and integrity for the job was the most insulting. Though I experienced a brief bout with disengagement and disappointment at the beginning of the school year, I never lost stride with my duties and always tended to my responsibilities even when massively overwhelmed with additional tasks.

With careful prayer, my next career move had been solidified. Most immediately, I would work to become an author. Each day of my 21-day fast was dedicated to writing a single devotional, hence the 21 days of devotion contained in this book. Because I lacked a solid resource that could get me through my tumultuous times at work, my mission was to create something that could serve as a go-to guide for the victims of workplace bullying, those who feel like their voice has been muted and made to feel invisible in a place where a sense of community should thrive. As I sacrificed sleep each morning to write this text, God gave me more assurance that this was all part of his plan. He's using my struggle to help other women see their way through their personal workplace pain.

Shortly after the completion of the first draft of this devotional, God's plan for my life was further revealed. Visions of my future shifted from glimmers to a clear picture. While preparing to transition out of my job, I would leverage my skill of communication to start my own business as a professional writer, speaker and success coach. My experiences could now help others revitalize their passion and purpose both in and out of their careers. I would utilize my certification in cognitive coaching obtained during graduate school and help other women to follow their passion in their life journey.

After sharing my God-given vision with my trusted circle of friends and family, I began getting booked for speaking engagements and even invested more time in ghostwriting for others. Other opportunities to coach women who faced similar job dissatisfaction emerged. My heart was filled with thankfulness. God was shifting me into my true purpose. Through these opportunities, my business manifested itself into what I now call Transformation7 by Tiffany A. Washington. The word transformation represents the change that must occur for anyone to fully walk inside of their purpose, and the number seven is the number of completion. God completely changed me in the process of my trial, much like the metamorphosis of a caterpillar into a butterfly. I started out moving slowly feeling unprotected from life's storms, but God molded me in the process so that I could take full flight and motivate others to do the same. Everything that I had experienced led me to an array of open doors. All I had to do was walk through them with confidence!

Prayer Changes Things

Prayer has certainly changed the trajectory of my life and the way in which I approach worklife roadblocks. Allow this devotional to do the same for you. Set aside dedicated time in the morning prior to the start of each workday, or devote some time at night before you go to sleep. This resource will even work if you need an extra boost during your lunch break. Whichever timeframe you decide, make it a sacred time for you and God.

As you read, you will find direction for each common situation faced while at work and receive targeted prayer to help navigate you through your toughest moments. You will receive empowerment, mental clarity, and internal strength to face any situation by reading this text. You will find practical, spiritual ways to deal with what is happening in the natural.

Women Winning at Work is separated into two sections. Each section navigates you on a journey to workplace sanity through devotion, reflection, and recording worklife worries that are further exposed by your personal work hag(s).

> **Section I – Devotion:** Use this section while spending consecrated time with God and your thoughts. The devotional section is broken into five parts that outline the stages of dealing with workplace woes. It also serves as a reminder of God's faithfulness to you and your Christian walk.
> **Section II – Reflection:** This section serves as an extended opportunity to synthesize your thoughts and further reflect on the word of God. Use this section to help you experience a deeper level of introspection as you arrive at conclusions regarding your worklife. Each devotional will ask questions, challenge you to think more deeply, and write your own prayers.

This devotional is your personal sunshine in the rain. If you are currently facing struggles at work, this devotional is for you. It's filled with poignant commentary, relevant workplace examples, and prayer that will help guide you through difficult worklife situations. Use this book as a platform for elevation. Stand firmly on the words contained within and let them shelter you from the turbulent winds of your own personal work hag (s).

Both veteran and novice workers alike have benefited from the consistent implementation of the commentary and prayers imbedded in this spiritual guide. Jackie, a workforce veteran from Houston, says, "This devotional can be read each morning to start your day on a positive note. I have my personal favorites that are earmarked for me to revisit regularly!"

Each day, feel free to go back and reread what resonates with you and apply it to your current situation. Do not delay your breakthrough by waiting or becoming complacent with your current work status with the same old work hag(s)! You must incorporate these devotionals daily to gain more peace and solitude while at work. Take control of your life now and conquer the issues that currently leave you feeling deflated. Fill your heart with God's continuous presence and watch your worklife soar!

All that you are currently experiencing shall soon pass away. Remember that it matters how you handle each situation. As you go through, ask God to reveal the lesson he has for you in this trial. There is *purpose* in the *process*. This devotional will guide you on how to move through worklife rough patches with grace. Make the decision to carry God with you daily. He has ordained this book for your hands. Be blessed, sister.

SECTION I PART I

ACKNOWLEDGE THE CHALLENGE

Worry does not yield resolution,
even when under attack.
Colliding with your naysayers, will
not bring your joy back.
So when you feel defeated at work
and want to throw in the towel,
Call on the name of Jesus and
rest with him for a while.

When you are Worried

"Be anxious for nothing, but in everything by prayer and supplication, with thanksgiving, let your requests be made known unto God; and the peace of God, which surpasses all understanding, will guard your hearts and minds through Christ Jesus."
(*New King James Version*, Phil. 4.6, 7)

"You can't pray and worry." These are the infamous words of my wise grandmother, and, I'm sure, many other wise women and men across the world. The two just don't go together. One must starve and the other must thrive. I predict that you will choose to pray and thrive. If such is the case, then you must know that prayer is not a fly-by-night operation for God. You must trust that he is steadily working on your behalf and hears your conversations with Him. God even talks back to you when your spirit is open to listening. His confirmation of your prayers may come in many forms including people, prophecy, or even while reading through your social media timeline! I have friends who have posted scriptures that speak directly to the prayers I have prayed assuring me that God heard my request.

While at work, you may have experienced creating a big presentation for the likes of upper-level management, vice-presidents, CEO's and owners. This alone can be nerve wrecking. Your immediate supervisor tells you, "There is a lot riding on this presentation." Being the perfectionist that you are, you pull out all the stops. You want to do an excellent job while simultaneously reassuring onlookers that you are the right person for the job. After all, you need this job. Better yet, you could even get a promotion if you do well! Placing this pressure on yourself can lead to sleepless nights, heart palpitations, and even an increase in blood pressure. You pray to God about the success of your presentation and you pretend to leave it in His hands. All the while, this gnawing voice replays in your head telling you that you have to get this just right in order to be recognized and noticed as a major player in the company.

When you remain anxious about matters that have already been lifted up to God, you laden yourself with undue stress and rob moments from your life! Instead, choose to live a life that makes your coworkers curious. In your daily walk, "Let your light to shine before men, that they may see your good works and glorify your Father in heaven" (Matt. 5.16). Worrying about the next promotion, your seemingly evil colleague, and other people's opinion of you will not get you any closer to the dreams and aspirations that God has placed on your heart. He is already in the process of answering that which you have uttered to Him. Shout with joyful thanksgiving for what He has promised to do on your behalf and allow peace to abound in your mind, body and spirit!

Pray this prayer when you are worried on the job:

Father in heaven, I come before you asking that you release me from the chains of my own worry while at work. What good is it to remain a slave to myself when you have already set the world free? I thank you right now that my worry is transforming into worship, and that my worship unto you will relieve me of the current stress I am experiencing. I praise your holy name for answered prayer, Lord! Thank you for hearing my prayer and answering in a way that best meets my needs and is aligned to your will. As I pray to you today, I ask that you replace any fear that I have with bold confidence. I can walk with authority on my job and throughout my career. I am reminded that "God has not given us a spirit of fear, but of power and of love and of a sound mind"(2 Tim. 1.7). You have given me all of the tools I need to thrive, Lord. Help me to see clearly that fear only assists me with falling. Comfort me in knowing that each request made to you is being answered expediently and will come at just the time I need it. I bless your name for positive outcomes in my life, and I thank you for reminding me that if you took care of me back then, you can certainly take care of me now. Thank you for peace and rest under your protective shield. In Jesus' name I pray, Amen.

1. **What is your specific workplace worry? What will help you give it to God?**

2. **Record your thoughts in the *Reflection Section*.**

When you are Under Attack

"Though I walk in the midst of trouble,
you will revive me;You will stretch out
Your hand against the wrath of my enemies,
andYour right hand will save me."
(Ps. 138.7)

When you find that the professional arena in which you work lacks employee cohesion and a sense of community, you may find yourself relegated to the option of operating inside of a bubble, an invisible barrier that protects you from the infamous work hags. Having to function this way on your job often leaves a less than palatable taste in your mouth. The danger of being in this bubble is revealed once co-workers' individual intentions start to outweigh the collective good of the company body. Even worse, your co-workers' personal appetites are fed in lieu of quelling the hunger of the collective organization. Thus, personal vicious attacks become inevitable and the bubble in which you've placed yourself soon bursts.

Let's take the example of people intentionally lying on you for personal career gain. In one of my worklife coaching sessions, my client, let's call her Lisa, expressed to me the experience of having a private conversation with other co-workers who then turned the context of the conversation around to appear as though Lisa had been speaking negatively about them. The group of co-workers teamed up against her and created a fictional story to tell their immediate supervisor. This led to Lisa being falsely accused of creating a negative work environment and participating in gossip. Written up for the incident, Lisa was in danger of losing her job. Later, she found out that the false reports were made because she held a coveted position that other workers envied. Sadly, this event tarnished her reputation, and she has spent time rebuilding her good name after ill-intentioned people tried to ruin what she worked so hard to build.

These unfortunate attacks rear their ugly head for what you may think is no good reason at all, but you must remember that there is always a root cause to human behavior. Though you may think you have done nothing wrong to deserve personal attacks, feelings of isolation, or ostracism, know that people operate in their own perceptions and truths.... even if those perceived truths are a lie!

Because you cannot make your colleagues behave in a manner that appeases your personal taste, choose instead to fill yourself with the word of God and remind yourself of what He promises. He shall not leave or forsake you, even in the midst of your trials. Because you belong to Him, you will not be defeated. Deuteronomy 28:7 tells you, "The Lord will cause your enemies who rise against you to be defeated before your face; they shall come out against you one way and flee before you seven ways." Praise God for His divine protection!

Pray this prayer when you feel attacked on the job:

> *Lord, I come before you with outstretched arms asking that you shine your face upon me so that I know that you are here. The struggle is real, and I am tempted to quit. Temper me, oh God, so that I may remain faithful to you even when I feel like I'm at the end of my rope at work. Wipe away my tears and frustrations and replace them with the peace that surpasses all understanding. I know that this situation is not my forever, but give me the strength to bear it with courage. Rejuvenate me, oh Lord, and cleanse my negative thoughts so that I may continue to be productive in this workspace. Eliminate the distraction of my own voice, and help me to more clearly hear yours. Teach me what I need to learn from this circumstance so that I may pass this test. Help me to move if you say move, and stand firm if that is your will for me at this time. Lead and guide me as I traverse this difficult path, and reassure me that you have not left my side. Change my attitude and approach toward work. Though I am facing tough times, Lord, allow me to remain positive and steadfastly seek your face for only you can bring me through this in the most graceful way. Deliver me, Lord, in the way you see fit. In Jesus' name I pray, Amen.*

1. **You may come under attack at work for many reasons that may not be immediately revealed. Think of a time you may have experienced personal attack.**

2. **In the *Reflection Section*, write about how you plan to or have already overcome workplace attacks.**

Colliding with Naysayers

"A fool's mouth is *his destruction, and*
his lips are *the snare of his soul."*
(Prov. 18.7)

One who consistently casts negative views is a naysayer. Each person in the world has probably encountered this unfortunate soul at some point in life's journey. When you collide with such people, it is paramount that you shield your spirit. Neglecting to do so will leave you vulnerable to unfavorable outcomes. The first line of defense against naysayers is to realize that negativity is much like an infection. Once it enters your body, only a doctor can assist with ridding you of the problem. Similarly, it takes God to move on the hearts of those who suffer from this pessimistic condition. Combat the onslaught of pessimism by staying in continuous prayer. Regular prayer helps you to respond to pessimists with calmness versus fury. The absence of prayer will lead you to react out of emotion rather than reply with love.

Even when you stay prayed up, it is also good practice to maintain allies on the job (or those who operate within your inner circle). I am reminded of a dear workplace friend who was a conscious ally in my often-troublesome place of work. During meetings, she supported me when I spoke up, gave ideas, headed up initiatives or had to go against the grain for the greater good of the students we served. She was also verbally assertive whenever I made presentations to the staff or even my principal.

When you have someone in your corner that purposely supports you, it gives others the permission to publicly back you as well. These are the people who will lift you up when you are faced with harsh criticism, rejection, or even incessant rudeness. Having a confidant, or at least someone you can trust with surface-level information, will ease the stress you may feel while walking through the situation. Should this not be an option, on Jesus you can depend! Retreat to your place of calm at work (your office, a small closet, your car) and seek Him for the solitude you need to make it through the day. Remember that naysayers are unavoidable creatures that roam this Earth. Pray that their hearts be softened while simultaneously guarding your own.

Pray this prayer when you experience workplace naysayers:

O mighty God, who holds all power in His hands, I come before your throne asking that you impart consistency upon me to regularly pray for the naysayer(s) in my life. Soften their hearts toward me and others. Overtake their negativity, and do not allow it to fester within my organization. Pull the toxicity out from the root and plant seeds of hope, encouragement, and kindness. When I am feeling frustrated by those who insist on infusing the workplace atmosphere with poisonous vibes, help me to quell my aggravation by lifting you up in my spirit. Take control of every circumstance that has the potential to brew negative deeds and replace them with positive actions that push others forward. Amen.

1. **If you have not already done so, consider the friend(s) on whom you can depend to stand with you in times of collision. How can you nurture those relationships and keep them strong?**

2. **Map out your answer in the *Reflection Section.***

When you feel Defeated

"Finally, my brethren, be strong in the Lord and in the power of His might. Put on the whole armor of God, that you may be able to stand against the wiles of the devil. For we do not wrestle against flesh and blood, but against principalities, against powers, against the rulers of the darkness of this age, against spiritual hosts of wickedness in the heavenly places. Therefore take up the whole armor of God, that you may be able to withstand in the evil day, and having done all, to stand."
(Eph. 6.10-13)

Consider the competitive nature of traditional jobs, especially in corporate America. Talks of upcoming promotions and newly created positions will send employees into a tailspin. Some even lose all sense of morals and ethics just to obtain what they perceive as something better. You, knowing you have earned an opportunity for promotion, put your name in the hat hoping for a chance at advancement, but your co-worker wants it more. They try to pummel you by using the method of slander and attacks on your character. Co-workers and workplace friends may even exploit your privately held conversations just to get ahead. People go for blood when promotion is involved. Unfortunately, sometimes the bloodshed is your own. These ploys are used as tactics for destruction. Initially these attacks may make you feel like the enemy has won, but we must be reminded to holdfast to God's hand.

When people's hearts are hardened with contempt, it's easy for you to become their prey. Devouring you like a roaring lion, the enemy leaves you feeling helpless, alone, and afraid. Scripture reminds us that we fight against powers much stronger than what we see in our own carnality. Thus, it is of the utmost importance to defeat those that war against us with the powerful weapon of the word. On your job, whether blue or white collar, feelings of defeat are inevitable. Some thrive on rendering another powerless, and others feed on intimidation and fear. Regardless of their fleshly ailment, you must stand strong and claim victory over defeat.

Work is a tough arena in which to exert your God-given power, especially in places where the presence of believers is not evident. However, war rages on if you so allow. Use the tools gifted to you by the Lord above to defeat those who take joy in your downfall. Stand on the promises of the word and seek God for deliverance from any ill that attempts to bind your greatness. Remember that the book of John tells us that the enemy comes but to steal, kill, and destroy. But God came so that you might have life, and have it more abundantly!

Pray this prayer when you are feeling defeated in the workplace:

Dear Lord, I come to you in the best way I know how, asking for your help during this trying time at work. This road is challenging, but I know you to be a deliverer. I implore you, Lord, as it is written in Psalms 59:1, "Deliver me from my enemies, O my God; Defend me from those who rise up against me." Give me the strength to stand firm on your holy word as I walk through this trial. Even though I see difficulty on my job, I declare that I will reign triumphant over my adversaries. They will not overtake my life. My spirit is strong, and my vision is clear. Because I am His child, I will not suffer defeat. Each experience I have is a training ground for the next season of my life. I will learn from each encounter and apply the teachings appropriately. I am victorious in the name of the Lord! These things I proclaim in Jesus' name. Amen.

1. **When things don't go the way we expect, we are often caught off guard, and it can take a while to regain ourselves. Reflect on how you can overcome feelings of defeat while at work.**

2. **Complete the questions in the *Reflection Section*.**

SECTION I PART II

SEEK GOD

You are perfectly imperfect, the
way God intended you to be.
When you are feeling undervalued
and unappreciated on the job,
He says, "Come see me."
Strive to get unstuck through His
validation and clarity through His eyes.
Find hope through your hurt, claim
your victory and your prize.

Perfectly Imperfect

"For we all stumble in many things. If anyone does not stumble in word, he is *a perfect man, able also to bridle the whole body."*
(Jas. 3.2)

Mistakes are often made, and for those keeping count of all your mishandlings, they are rarely forgotten. What you must remember is that mistakes serve as training ground for your mental and spiritual growth. Without them, you remain the same – stagnant – never actualizing your God-given potential. Mental acuity is necessary for the path that God chooses for us, and that acuity is refined each time an error is made and then corrected. Though we strive to follow God's word to a tee, we all fall short. But, because we are God's children, we know that our imperfections in executing the word are perfected through Christ.

Consider the age-old example of a young child touching something hot. The little one's reaction is to immediately pull his hand back and say, "Hot." As the child continues to learn the difference between what's safe and what's not, his ability to think is heightened. He processes before he touches and has learned that certain objects project more heat than he wants to feel.

Transfer the previous example into the workplace. It's your first time working on a large account within the firm. Your job is to make the company money with each new client brought onto the team. Because the higher-ups believe that you show promise, they give you this large account in hopes to see you soar. During the weekly company meeting, you find out that your client has backed out of the deal because of your insufficient knowledge about the clients' products and offerings.

Embarrassed, you excuse yourself from the meeting to go and sulk and beat yourself up over the mistake. In the following days, your work hag decides to criticize your ability to cut it in this field, and openly talks about you in front of your boss and other workers. You fear that your work ethic may not cut it and contemplate taking on a less challenging job at a different firm. Doubt creeps in and steals your confidence.

Two weeks later, you are given another client, and because you are determined not to make the same blunder twice, you spend days doing your research before sealing the deal with the new customer. You read, ask questions, and go the extra mile to learn new information. After exhibiting fierce determination, you have a great encounter with the client. At the next company meeting, you are praised for being efficient, and the customer mentions how pleased they were with your level of service.

In this example, you can clearly see that mistakes bring about growth and knowledge. Let us not be hesitant to take action because of fear. You are ever evolving, ever-changing and growing. Once you realize that you have stopped experiencing mental and spiritual enlightenment, take some time with God to get back on track and make more mistakes....

Pray this prayer when you are remorseful or fearful about making mistakes on the job:

Lord, thank you for allowing me to see the blessings in my mistakes. Help me to understand that any blunder I make can be used for my own personal growth and learning. Instead of being embarrassed or fearful, Lord, remind me of the good news that I am perfected through you, Christ Jesus! Only you are perfect, Father, but walking in your way perfects me! When I see that my neighbor / work colleague persecutes me for my mistakes, propel me forward with gladness for I know that I live not to honor man, but to glorify you. Let my life be a testament to your dwelling within me, and allow my missteps to morph me into a bolder believer, willing to walk through life fearlessly for you are always with me. Thank you, Lord, for your redeeming blood that washes away all of my sins even when I mess up! Forgiveness is a gracious gift from God, and I ask for and accept it fully when I sin against you. Thank you, God, for my imperfections and your saving grace. Amen.

1. **Reflect on how you have recovered from a mistake you made at work. What steps did you take to rectify the mistake? How did God show up to guide you through the situation?**

2. **Record your thoughts in the *Reflection Section.***

Feeling Undervalued and Unappreciated

"You were bought at a price; do not become slaves of men."
(1 Cor. 7.23)

Various fields of work are often thankless and overlooked. Supervisors rarely pat you on the back or acknowledge your hard work and effort. You put your blood, sweat, and tears into projects-relentlessly combing through every detail until the outcome is perfect. Sleep is sacrificed, weekends are spent at the computer, and when friends ring your phone, you press ignore because you have to please the thankless boss or cover for the less than stellar work of your peers. You have devoted yourself to tending every aspect of your career, but no one notices–and it seems like no one cares. The good news is that you are not the only one feeling this way. This situation was not designed just for you.... This is called life. What makes all the difference in the world is how you choose to respond.

When you need reassurance, reflect on the experiences of the Lord. Think of all the miracles Jesus performed and the work He did to save souls. This man literally walked among crowds, yet some still did not realize his greatness! Can you imagine having the power to heal but still be condemned, the power to save but still be ignored, or the power to feed thousands with limited resources but still be doubted by the world? These wonderful acts remind us that if the Lord continued in His greatness despite being overlooked by many, you should also continue to do your best work regardless of recognition.

The work of your hands is ordained by Christ. The validation you seek comes from Him. Man may give you a "good job" or an "atta boy" for individual tasks, but God gives you the ultimate "well done" after reviewing the entirety of your life just before you enter the gates of heaven! Your final reward is greater than the accolades of any man. Though they are an honor to receive (especially tangible trophies and awards to commemorate your success), they do not compare to the eternity that God gives you in return for your service here on Earth. Until that time comes, pat yourself on the back and reaffirm your faith in Him. He will honor you with the best reward of all...everlasting life!

When you are feeling undervalued and unappreciated at work, pray this prayer:

I come to you, Lord Jesus, with an open heart. Fill it with contentment even when I feel like my work goes unnoticed. When I find myself feeling low and undervalued, give me the rise I need to continue on, working with the same confidence you exhibited during your time here on earth. Affirm me, oh Lord, and let me know that the work I do is an asset. Give me the strength to carry on even when no one shows appreciation to me. However, Lord, deliver me when the time is right so that I might gain access into places that make me feel good about what I do. Control the atmosphere of my current job and transform it into a place that treats others with the recognition and respect they deserve. Relax the environment so that peace can be found while working. Remove any contempt that I may be breeding and replace it with a willingness to complete all that is before me. In Jesus' name, Amen.

1. **Reflect on how God validates you each day. How has His goodness towards you made you feel both valued and appreciated?**

2. **Be sure to record your answers in the *Reflection Section*.**

Getting Unstuck

"... but we also glory in tribulations, knowing that tribulation produces perseverance; and perseverance, character; and character, hope."
(Rom. 5.3, 4)

When life occurs, we put our foot in our mouth, stay at a job well past our prime, commit to uninspiring tasks, overextend ourselves physically and emotionally, outgrow the work we once use to love, and begrudgingly devote ourselves to something we absolutely hate. We just get...stuck. Of course, it's easy to get stuck in the mud without the Lord. For some of us, it has happened before – you step in a puddle thinking that you are going to lift your foot right out of it. Instead, your shoe gets stuck and may even come off. Now you are shoeless, and your foot is even further exposed to the elements.

What do you do? You bend over, pull your shoe out of the mud, hope that it's still salvageable, and either slide it back on your foot after flinging the mud away or walk with one shoe on and the other off until you reach your desired destination. What you don't do is abandon your whole foot because it was unsuspectingly caught in the mud. Just like we have faith that the sullied shoe still has some value, God also shows this same regard to us. He picks us up, cleans us off, and places us back on our feet to continue the journey.

When striving to get unstuck while in your career, remember your own innate ability to wiggle your way out. You have the knowledge, the intellect, and the wherewithal to maneuver out of whatever issue you face. If you are sick of reporting to a job every day, you have the power to change the outcome. Commit to finding a new job that is a better fit with your current goals.

Perhaps you don't know exactly what you want your next step to be, but you are currently uninspired at work. Start by honing in on your God-given talents. Have you strengthened them enough to step into your own business? If not, are you prepared to invest in more education or courses that will develop you professionally? Whether you are dissatisfied at work or at a crossroads on what to do next, God has equipped you with all that is needed to get unstuck. Utilize the resources available to you and release yourself from the entrapment in which you are entangled.

Pray this prayer when you feel stuck in your current career:

Lord God, release me from my own thoughts of being stuck right where I am. Life is constantly changing, moving and stretching my ability to persevere. I proclaim that I am not stuck, rather, I am quickly accruing all of my resources so that I can transition into a different place in my thoughts, my actions, and even my career. I know that you will never leave me nor forsake me, Lord. I thank you for being my support as I use what you have gifted me to shift that which I can control. Help me to do the work of becoming unstuck, and allow me to see progress at each turn. Amen.

1. **How will you choose to get unstuck? List three actionable steps to get you on the road to clarity.**

2. **Record your action steps in the *Reflection Section.***

Finding Hope through Hurt

"Be of good courage, And He shall strengthen your heart, All you who hope in the Lord."
(Ps. 31.24)

It's challenging to be hopeful when your heart is weighed down with disappointment. Setbacks at work due to another person trying to taint your career can deliver an unexpected blow. Moreover, peer gossip, personal vendettas, demotions, and being treated as inferior by your supervisor are all hurts that are tough to overcome. When you find yourself injured in such a fashion, trust that there is hope, BUT you must be fearless and boldly face these hindrances with positivity. This can be done easily with the help of God.

Take the example of Hagar, a slave in the house of Abraham and Sarah, husband and wife. Sarah could not bear children, an embarrassing reality during biblical times. Because of her remorse for not being able to give Abraham a son, she convinced him to use Hagar as a surrogate. Abraham agreed, and conceived with Hagar. Once Sarah saw that Hagar was pregnant, she became resentful and despised the very presence of Hagar. She began to act as Hagar's real-life work hag. Sarah mistreated Hagar so much that she cast

Hagar and her son into the wilderness. While there, an angel came to Hagar promising that the Lord would make her unborn son, Ishmael, the father of a great nation.

Although Hagar was abused and sent away, God quickly rectified the situation. She was instructed to go back to the home of Abraham and Sarah where she would live peacefully for another thirteen years. She then moved on to raise her child who ruled nations (Gen. 16). Because of her trust, God blessed Hagar and her descendants. She truly found hope through a hurtful situation and reaped the benefits that God had for her life.

Think about each time God has delivered you from a circumstance that you were certain would knock you down. Though the situation took on high winds and it seemed as if a tornado had blown through your life, you found yourself on the other side, slightly bruised, but still standing. Reflecting on the depths of your past is reason enough to have hope for your future! Whenever I go through a trial, my mother always reassures me by saying, "Today is not your final destination." Let these words be of comfort as you walk through life. Today is not your forever. Walk through this season with confidence knowing that with God everything will work for your good.

Pray this prayer when you need to find hope while at work:

Heavenly Father, sometimes my workdays seem more difficult than what I can handle. In these moments, instill within me the power to move forward with authority. Lord, let me not run from my worklife adversity; rather, give me the courage to press my way through. Your word, Romans 8:25, tells me that if we hope for what we do not see, we eagerly wait for it with perseverance. Allow me to keep faith and wait on that which I cannot touch. I proclaim victory and not defeat. I claim resilience and not inflexibility. I declare that my hurts will only prepare me for the greater that you have for my life. Thank you, Lord, for hope and patience. I will not bow down and hang my head in sorrow as if I have no hope. You, oh Lord, have brought me through each trial, and I depend on you to do the same at this juncture of my career. I praise your name for the manifestation of positive outcomes. Mend me where I am broken. Cleanse all of my wounds. Wash my heart and renew my vigor and vitality. These things I ask in Jesus' name, Amen.

1. **What *hurt* have you had to overcome in order to be *hopeful* about your worklife? What growth have you seen within yourself as a result of getting past the pain?**

2. **Use the *Reflection Section* to think about your journey.**

SECTION I PART III

FIND PEACE THROUGH HIM

Take heart in knowing that you are not alone.
Find peace and comfort in your earthly home.
Carry forth His light. Be the beacon that shines.
God has all of the good stuff to
make your life divine.
Though worklife edges may be jagged,
and discontentment fills your heart, may
the peace you gain never depart.

I AM NOT ALONE

"And the Lord, He is the One who goes before you. He will be with you, He will not leave you nor forsake you; do not fear nor be dismayed."
(DEUT. 31.8)

Whether you are attempting to climb the corporate ladder and your attempts are thwarted unexpectedly, you are unfulfilled with your current position, or you are confused about your next career step, God is always there to guide your daily process. Sometimes, when things don't fall into place as you feel they should, common feelings of frustration and doubt arise, and you begin to wonder if God is even witnessing the current situation. In your vocational journey, you may have experienced ostracism and exclusion by your peers, a demotion, or even workplace bullying. Please know that these apparent failures are only stepping stones to your greater destiny. You will soon realize that each workplace trial equips you for the next level of elevation.

While nimbly steering your way through the career obstacle course, it is important to note how worklife experiences mirror that of a foggy drive to work. Imagine that during your morning commute, a dense fog advisory has been issued via your local weather authority. Alone in your car, you realize that dense fog decreases visibility, thereby stifling the pace at which you normally drive. Anxiety heightens and a range of pressured thoughts race through your head. Will I make it to work on time? I hope no one hits me. How can I make up for the time that I miss if I am late because of this weather?

In many cases of heavy fog, you can't see the car lights in front of you – so you become more vigilant and tense, and you may even have to drive at a snail's pace to safely reach your destination. The beautiful thing about this experience is that you can see God in it! Though your route was altered by weather conditions, you still made it! You drove defensively and arrived to work safely. The same applies with God. He will safely lead your journey through life, navigating your path while purposely choosing how quickly or slowly you will meet your desired destination. If you take a moment to reflect on all that you have persevered, you will realize that God has been with you at every step. Even when you can't see your way at work, God is always there. All you have to do is call on Him.

Pray this prayer when you feel alone at your place of work:

> *Lord, I thank you that even when I feel alone, you are right there. Cloak me in peace. Wrap and cradle me in your arms. I find comfort in feeling your presence. Help me to know that I can live with joy each day because I am yours; therefore, I am never alone. Give me the unction to make a decision to dwell in joy even when my days seem foggy and my coworkers have abandoned me. I praise your name because your presence never leaves me. Lord, when I falter and have doubt that you are near, reassure me with confirmation as only you can. The work of the day can sometimes be a lonesome winding road with unexpected surprises on every turn. Go before me, Lord, and stand by me. In your mighty name I pray. Amen.*

1. **What other techniques might you use when feeling alone at work that also support your relationship with God?**

2. **Head over to the *Reflection Section* to record your thoughts.**

Finding Peace

"Peace I leave with you, My peace I give to you; not as the world gives do I give to you. Let not your heart be troubled, neither let it be afraid."
(John 14.27, 28)

"These things I have spoken to you, that in Me you may have peace. In the world you will have tribulation; but be of good cheer, I have overcome the world."
(John 16.33)

Anxiety, a common added stress to workers around the world, can have detrimental effects on the heart, mind, and body. Moreover, some even suffer from panic attacks that envelop them with an impending sense of doom and death. Though this illness is medically diagnosed, people experience the aforementioned regularly and don't realize the symptoms are a result of stress. Do you find yourself worried over every detail of your life? Do you feel like you have to know what's around each corner so that you can control the outcome? Have you ever felt powerless when you cannot control how others respond or react to you or something that involves you?

If you answered yes to any of these questions, God wants you to stop trying to figure everything out and allow Him to have His perfect way. When we ask for God's will for our lives, it means that we lay aside our own personal projections about how our life should be and give over the control that we so desperately feel we need. Apprehensive behavior gives way to doubt and yields itself to fear. It's okay for some things to remain unknown. We must rejoice, for God has the ultimate plan, and it will not fail! Today, set your mind at ease by praying and offering thanksgiving to the most high. You will find that His peace washes you, cleanses you, gives you mental clarity, and calms you even in the center of your difficulty.

Pray this prayer when you need peace at work:

> *Lord, I come to you today wanting to release the anxiety I have over things that I cannot currently control. Help me to release all unnecessary burdens. You tell me in your word to cast all of my care upon you because you care for me. As I cast my care, Lord, grant me the peace that you promise. Help me to move forward with a renewed mind and a refreshed view on life. Allow me the opportunity to enjoy each day without worrying about what will happen tomorrow. While I'm at work, Lord, fill my heart with your presence so that the calamity that surrounds me may not distract me. Abound in my spirit and engulf me with your steadfast assurance. I thank you right now for hearing my request and answering swiftly. Let me see evidence of this answered prayer through my increased level of calm, comfort, and confidence in you. These things I ask in Jesus' name, Amen.*

1. **Challenge: Create your own prayer for peace. What do you want to request of God?**

2. **Record your prayer in the *Reflection Section.***

Walking in the Light of God

"Let your light so shine before men,
that they may see your good works and
glorify your Father in heaven."
(Matt. 5.16)

In the workplace, surely darkness eventually falls upon your head. Dark ominous clouds come in the form of people who rain down negativity. The foreboding spirits you sometimes encounter can easily attempt to steal light from a sunny day, but they shall not prosper. Fortunately, you are the light that overcomes darkness. Notice that even on a day of severe weather, the sky gets dark yet the sun shines. Though overcast skies are present, not a day goes by where the sun doesn't make its grand entrance.

Let's examine the biblical story of Ruth. She was a widow who, after losing her husband, chose to follow her mother-in-law Naomi, also a widow, back to her hometown. Though the situation was bleak, Ruth knew that she needed the support of her mother-in-law. In light of their lives without husbands, Naomi instructed Ruth on how to survive and work to gather food. Ruth went to a local field and modestly gathered left over grains behind the harvesters. Once Boaz, the owner of the field, noticed Ruth and her humble nature, he immediately began to look after her and protect her. Boaz noticed something different about Ruth, causing him to shine favor upon her even though she did not have permission to be in his field. As the story of Ruth progresses, we find out that the young widow, who suffered great loss, is restored through the kindness of Boaz. They go on to marry and have a son with the help of Naomi (Ruth 1-3).

Just like Ruth, as a believer, you have a duty and responsibility to shine brightly so that humankind may be drawn unto you...even in the work place. That gravitational pull of others in your direction is the light of God. Carry it with you daily, for light always trumps darkness. On this worklife journey, you will have unsavory human interaction. Through it all, remember that you are a disciple of Christ, a representative for the most high, and His unique precious creation. Represent Him well.

Pray this prayer when you need God's light to be revealed within you while at work:

> *Heavenly Father, I come before you today asking that you hide me behind the cross. Let others see you dwelling within my spirit daily. Help me to remember that I am your unique creation set apart from the ways of the world. As I encounter others with ill intent or indecent attitudes, decrease my personal will to respond as those of the world would. Instead, allow me to recall how you responded to naysayers during the time that you walked this Earth. Lord, extinguish any desires that I may have to lash out at others and increase my level of patience with those who surround me each day. Let your love and light radiate through me as rays of sunshine just as Ruth's aura overtook Boaz. Overwhelm me with your goodness and mercy so that I may share your good news with others through my walk and my talk. Elevate me to a new level of humbleness as I go before people who need more of you and find it through me. Allow me to serve as a beacon for your glory while in my place of work. Thank you for hearing my prayer, Lord. Amen.*

1. **What else might you add to the outlined prayer in order to cover your need to walk in the light of God?**

2. **Write your prayer in the *Reflection Section.***

God Is Where the Good Stuff Is

"Finally, brethren, whatever things are true, whatever things are *noble, whatever things* are *just, whatever things* are *pure, whatever things* are *lovely, whatever things* are *of good report, if* there is *any virtue and if* there is *anything praiseworthy – meditate on these things."*
(Phil. 4.8)

Stuff – a word describing things that cannot otherwise be identified in a singular and specific fashion. Frequently, we use this word when asking questions.... What is all this stuff? We also choose to classify a massive pile of objects as stuff.... Why is there so much stuff on your desk? Finally, when we become completely overwhelmed, we *stuff* things into drawers and closets so that we won't be reminded of all the junk we actually have. Eventually we accumulate so much *stuff* that we forget certain items' original state of being prior to the *stuff*. Be reminded that although you get bombarded with your own *stuff*, God is truly where the good *stuff* resides. Be sure to find Him in every life circumstance.

Challenge yourself to revisit your most recent obstacle. Maybe it was a refusal from your manager after requesting to attend a training that you thought would accelerate your career. Though you were hesitant about asking in the first place, receiving that training would not have only bolstered your on-the-job enjoyment, it also would have made you more marketable for future opportunities and helped you to grow other colleagues within your current work environment by bringing the information back and training others.

Being given an opportunity to spend time away from the job to hone your skills was just what you needed to rejuvenate your worklife spirit. Once your supervisor said no, you could literally feel your heart drop and both sadness and frustration ensued. You carry the weight of your supervisor's denial with you and add it to the pile of *stuff* that has been overwhelming you at work.

How many layers of trouble or discourse are you willing to peel back in order to find God in the midst of your rejection? After removing the outer layer of intimidation, the next layer of dissatisfaction, the following layer of unhappiness, the fourth layer of discouragement and the fifth layer of rejection, you will find God and all of His nobility at the core holding everything together. So, at the crux of you trying to find God, know that He will always be there beneath all the *stuff* you choose to give authority. His word tells us to think on the good things, and that always starts with Him.

Pray this prayer when you need to see the face of God and His goodness while at work:

Heavenly Father, you have instructed me to think on those things that are pure, holy and praiseworthy. As I journey through each day of my worklife, open my eyes to your goodness in spite of the clutter of my job. Open my heart, and make me fully aware of your perfect works. Remind me that there is no power in the extraneous stuff that crowds my life. Deliver me from any thoughts that are not like your thoughts and ways that do not mirror your ways. Thank you in advance for rescuing me from the snares of my own mind. I choose not to be trapped within the layers of my life that have already been taken care of by you. Free me from myself and bless me with the ability to think on the positive things happening in my life with you at the core. Replace any negative thoughts I may have with thoughts of your mercy and grace. Thank you, Lord. Amen.

1. **Challenge: Consider all the blessings God has provided in your life. List the most recent worklife blessing that surely could not have been achieved without the help of the Lord.**

2. **Head over to the *Reflection Section* and write your thoughts.**

SECTION I PART IV

CHANGE YOUR PERSPECTIVE

As you transition from fear to faith,
much strength you shall find
From turning the other cheek and praying
your way through troublesome times.
Practice the fruits of the spirit
every chance you get,
For one does not receive a second
chance to clean-up his first regret.

From Fear to Faith

"He who dwells in the secret place of the Most High Shall abide under the shadow of the Almighty. I will say of the Lord, 'He is my refuge and my fortress; My God, in Him I will Trust.' Surely He shall deliver you from the snare of the fowler and from the perilous pestilence. He shall cover you with His feathers, and under His wings you shall take refuge; His truth shall be your shield and buckler.You shall not be afraid of the terror by night, nor of the arrow that flies by day, nor of the pestilence that walks in darkness, nor of the destruction that lays waste at noonday. A thousand may fall at your side, and ten thousand at your right hand; But it shall not come near you."
(Ps. 91.1-7)

Operating in fear only satisfies the comfort in which you want to reside, and much to our dismay, life is not always comfortable, nor has God promised it to be. Experiences in your everyday worklife may present war-like challenges that bruise you in ways you never would have imagined. People may use carnal weapons such as the tongue that pierces like a dagger as verbal abuse, or cutthroat tactics. When these obstacles are faced, you must look at them as opportunities to grow in faith. As outlined in the scripture, it is blatantly clear that hunters will come against you, seeking their prey. Yet, God has promised to both protect and deliver us. What good news!

So, you made a mistake on your job. The effects of your blunder seem to be endless. Both you and your coworkers have to go back and redo or undo work that you previously completed incorrectly. To make matters worse, you must endure the pain of starting a project over all while putting up with constant eye-rolling, nearly inaudible grumblings and deep sighs of discontent from your not-so gracious workmates. You fear what your manager might say to you about the incident and how you have slowed down the productivity of all of your peers. Singlehandedly, you have created a crash and burn moment. Certainly, you will be demoted for this imposition or at least handed down some type of consequence. What if your manager decides to pull work away from you repeatedly until you finally have nothing to do when you come to work? What if that leads to a layoff...all because of one error?

As you pray today, remember that even when facing hurdles that seem to impede the ease with which you flow through the day, it matters how you face each situation. Will you cower in disappointment and shame? Will you lash out and act unprofessionally, scarring your own reputation? OR will you decide to rise like a champion and dwell in the presence of the Lord while allowing Him to fight your battle? In this moment, choose to sustain less injury and pain and invite the Lord's abiding presence to prevail.

Pray this prayer when you are feeling fearful at work:

Lord, I beseech thee and ask that you hear my call. Your word says that you are my refuge and security. Place peace in my heart; for I know that even during my storm, you are always here to protect me. Let me not walk in fear but in the power and authority that has already been bestowed upon me by your gracious hand. When I am treated cruelly on the job, help me to turn the other cheek and come to you in prayer. Thank you, Lord, for reminding me in your word that the weapons with which I fight "...are not carnal but mighty in God for pulling down strongholds" (2 Cor. 10.4). Strengthen me where I am weak, Lord, so that I may endure until the end. I have faith that you will bring me the peace and joy that I seek as long as I stay inside of your will. Hear my prayer, oh Lord. Amen.

1. **What are some ways that you can overcome fear at work?**

2. **Provide detailed thoughts in the *Reflection Section.***

TURNING THE OTHER CHEEK

"But I say to you who hear: Love your enemies, do good to those who hate you, bless those who curse you, and pray for those who spitefully use you. To him who strikes you on the one cheek, offer the other also. And from him who takes away your cloak, do not withhold your tunic either."
(LUKE 6.27-29)

Oftentimes, turning a deaf ear and a blind eye to people who wrong us on the job is more than a notion. The flesh wants what it wants and revenge or payback with word or deed is the effortless retort. Your Lord and savior, Jesus Christ, is the shining example of turning the other cheek, also known as walking in love or even better – forgiveness. Take your own life for example. How often has God forgiven you, had mercy on you, or thrown your past sins into the sea of forgetfulness just because you asked?

Take this a step further and apply the biblical story of Judas, the ultimate work hag. He was one of the twelve disciples, one of the followers of Christ. Just before the last supper, Judas caught wind of the high priest's plan to arrest and kill Jesus. Without thought, Judas made his way to the chief priests and offered to hand over Jesus in exchange for thirty pieces of silver. He agreed to keep watch for the perfect time to arrest Jesus. Though the Lord knew that Judas would betray him, he still allowed Judas to commune with him and the disciples on the day of the last supper. Shortly after the supper, while Jesus was meeting with his disciples in Gethsemane, Judas led a small crowd of men with swords and clubs to detain Jesus. Judas kissed Jesus on the cheek as a sign to the chief priests that the man he kissed was the one to be carried off to jail (Matt. 26.14-16). Jesus acknowledged that Judas came to have him arrested, and Jesus went with the crowd peacefully without lashing out at Judas, for he knew that the scripture had to be fulfilled and that he must die for the sins of the world.

Wouldn't it be great to have such grace in the face of workplace trouble? Even though Jesus knew that he would be betrayed, he kept his calm and went on to fulfill his calling. To be clear, God also wants us to use wisdom; we should not allow people to repeatedly take advantage of us and not speak up for ourselves. However, we should not be reactionary in our dealings with individuals whose sole purpose may be to do us harm. Walking away humbly is a task with which we are charged, especially when facing dilemmas with peers and colleagues. Maintaining peace while working with others are tough waters to navigate, but you must sail through the choppy sea until you make it to shore. When enemies come against you like a flood, put your rain gear on and weather the storm.

Pray this prayer for the ability to turn the other cheek in the workplace:

Father, when I am faced with the charge of turning the other cheek, please allow me to do so gracefully, for I am a reflection of you, and you are the ultimate giver of grace. Stir up the strength that resides within me, and give me the ability to practice restraint when communicating with others at work who may have ill intentions toward me. Subdue my flesh, Lord, so that I may gratify you with my actions toward others in the midst of their wrongdoing. Rain down your love on me, so that I too can show love to my foes. Deliver me from evil, Lord, and deliver those around me who may be wrestling with demons and strongholds. Help them to see your face through my daily walk and the light that I carry each day. This I ask in Jesus' name. Amen.

1. **In the flesh, going tit-for-tat with your adversary may be gratifying, but this is a fleeting moment. What instances have you had to practice what God said and turn the other cheek? How did the situation ultimately resolve?**

2. **Write about it in the *Reflection Section*.**

Pray your Way

"Now this is the confidence that we have in Him, that if we ask anything according to His will, He hears us. And if we know that He hears us, whatever we ask, we know that we have the petitions that we have asked of Him."
(1 John 5.14, 15)

There is an age-old adage stating, "Prayer changes things." Millions of us know this to be true because we have seen God work and move in our lives. Think about it for a moment...you have been delivered from difficult circumstances, felt the power of the Holy Spirit, and recovered from illness and escaped near death experiences all because you prayed for yourself or someone prayed for you. The key to continuing to see blessings like the aforementioned manifest in our lives is to pray without ceasing, make our requests known unto God, and then thank Him continuously for the answered prayer. Once you have done everything in your power to withstand the trials that occur on your job, prayer must be what you stand on. Allow prayer to comfort you, support you, and uplift you.

At times when we are going through difficulty, we tend to rest in sad places, feeling down for ourselves and walking around hopeless. In other instances, we try to put on a good face for those around us, but we are languishing in depression on the inside or tormenting ourselves in private. The awesome thing about prayer is that you can use it as a weapon to combat any obstacle along your faith walk. Once you incorporate prayer into your daily life, you will find that it uplifts you, eases heartache, decreases stress, and motivates you to move forward with confidence. Remember that prayer is your personal conversation with God. You speak, He listens. You listen, He speaks.

Be mindful that designated prayer time will help you to focus on God and tune out everything else. Create space for prayer and declutter your time. Empty all things that distract you from getting close to God. Once you find this space, or the "sweet spot" as I like to call it, use it to be vulnerable with God. While at work, remove yourself from the noisy chatter by going to your office/cubicle/classroom/car or an area that does not have much traffic and dedicate that space to Him. You may even find yourself outside under a tree!

Wherever you find your sacred space, pour out your spirit and let him fill you up with His joy. During this time, you can quote scripture, putting Him in remembrance of His word, and meditate on His goodness. You may also visualize the day you would like to have and commit those thoughts to Him so that He can guide you in achieving that visualization, or you can read something inspirational and pray about what you have read. Also, do not forget to pray for your work hag. They need Jesus, too!

Any situation you encounter always has a solution. Pray, ask for confirmation, and listen for the answer. Be prepared for your confirmation to come in unexpected formats such as through a song, a person affirming prayers that you did not even share, or immediate changes to your current situation. Go forth with expectation and trust in the Lord without doubting His power. Walk boldly. Stand firm. Believe that He is working to answer your prayers.

Pray this prayer to cover any workplace situation:

Lord God, I come to you with a humble spirit, asking that you deliver me from anything that may hinder me from being my best self. Whether it be at work or in my personal life, place me on the right track and help me to walk completely in your will. Help me to understand that each trial that I face benefits my growth and strength to have more faith in you. Give me a conquering spirit, Father. With you, I know that I can triumph over the enemy and slay any dragon that may come against me because I am equipped with the power of your word. Bless me inside of my current workplace territory. Through your holy name, empower me with the courage to walk in the authority that you have imparted on me. Because I am your child, I know that each place I go is blessed. Every road I travel is blessed. The people with whom I interact are blessed, and those who reside over me are blessed through my gifts and talents. As I walk through each facet of life, endow me with your Holy Spirit and allow me to feel your presence. When I am scared, lonely, weak, hopeless, or under duress, remind me that I am safe in your bosom. You hide me from the center of the storm and bring me respite when it's time to rest and courage when it's time to face my fears. In you, Lord, there is matchless power that I can tap into at any time. Thank you for an open invitation to call upon your name whenever I am in need, or just to simply praise you! In your word, you command me to "Ask, and it will be given to you; seek, and you will find; knock, and it will be opened to you" (Matt. 7.7). Lord, I come before you asking, seeking, and knocking. Hear my prayer and receive it into your chamber. I believe that you have good things in store for me, and I leave my arms open ready to accept all the blessings you have carved out for me. I love you, Lord. In Jesus' name I pray. Amen.

1. **Challenge: Write your best prayer to God. Have it to encompass each obstacle you are currently facing at work. Talk to Him about everything that troubles you. After completion, leave it in God's hands and continuously proclaim the victory over your trials.**

2. **Record your all-inclusive prayer in the *Reflection Section.***

Practicing the Fruits

"But the fruit of the Spirit is love, joy, peace, longsuffering, kindness, goodness, faithfulness, gentleness, self-control. Against such there is no law."
(Gal. 5.22, 23)

Walking in the spirit is no easy task, especially at work. When faced with the temptation to "read someone their rights" or "tell them where they can go," it's rather hard to remind yourself to walk in love! Maybe one of your workmates decides to speak to you harshly, demanding that a task gets completed. Even though she is not your superior, she takes pride in telling you and others what to do. Her tone towards you is that of a parent to a child. Frustrated, your brain starts to formulate all of the daggers your mouth will toss as soon as she closes hers. The moment you tell that coworker exactly how you feel and what's on your mind, your body probably tingles with satisfaction. A smile may even dance on your face. There is a pleasing sensation that covers your body when you put her in her place, but this is so displeasing to God. When you slay others with your tongue, you are unconsciously starving the fruits of the spirit.

Remind yourself of the scripture in John 15:4, 5 that commands that you "Abide in Me, and I in you. As the branch cannot bear fruit of itself, unless it abides in the vine, neither can you, unless you abide in Me. I am the vine, you are the branches. He who abides in Me, and I in him, bears much fruit; for without Me you can do nothing." This scripture clearly illustrates that Jesus is the vine, the one who sustains you and allows fruit to come forth. Further, the scripture also reveals that branches on the vine that do not bear fruit are taken away.

Do not banish your branch into nonexistence due to lack of self-control. Allow yourself to be pruned so that you can produce more fruit. Of course, this means practicing each fruit of the spirit daily, taming your tongue, bringing your fleshly desires under submission, and withstanding all obstacles you encounter. Reap the benefits of practicing the fruits in your life: *love, joy, peace, long-suffering, kindness, goodness, faithfulness, gentleness and self-control.* Through them, you can never go wrong.

Pray this prayer when it becomes hard to practice the fruits of the spirit at work:

> *Lord, help me to walk in your ways and acknowledge your governance over my life. If I am a reflection of you, I must show it in thought, word, deed and action. When it gets tough to bite my tongue or treat someone with kindness, nudge me in the right direction. Bring my flesh under submission that I might not sin against you knowingly. Take away my need for self-gratification, and propel me into a state of perpetual giving. Though practicing the fruits is a challenge on my job, give me the strength to give the opposite of what I sometimes receive. When I am given hatred, Lord, allow me to show love. As sorrow fills the hearts of colleagues, help me to bring them joy. In the midst of disorganization and chaos, let me find peace. When the days seem long and the turmoil is great, help me to practice longsuffering. When people give me rudeness, let me offer up kindness. When evil is lurking at the corner, I will combat it with goodness. When workers give less than their best, I will remain faithful to the duties for which I have been hired. When employees approach me in harsh and abrupt manners, I will temper my spirit and answer in a gentle tone. Finally, Lord, when I have the urge to curse someone with my words or have an outburst of anger, allow me to practice self-control. These things I ask in Jesus' name. Amen.*

1. **Which fruit do you have the most trouble practicing at work? What actions will you actively commit to so that the troublesome fruit can be made stronger in your life?**

2. **Head over to the *Reflection Section* to outline your thoughts.**

SECTION I PART V

ENJOY THE JOURNEY

Quicken your hands to do the work of the day
and walk it out if on this path you must stay.
Enjoy the journey of this given life
while promoting positivity and not strife.
Enter His courts with thanksgiving
and give Him praise,
for He will make your path straight
in His own special way.

Being Productive

"Whatever your hand finds to do, do it *with your might; for there* is *no work or device or knowledge or wisdom in the grave where you are going."*
(Eccles. 9.10)

"He who is slothful in his work is a brother to him who is a great destroyer."
(Prov. 18.9)

You are here on assignment, destined for a mighty purpose with a divine call. Let not the workplace in which you currently reside be found in shambles due to your personal negligence. Research shows that more than 70% of people in this nation dislike some portion of their job. A good friend of mine, let's call her Gina, fell into this category. She allowed her disdain for the job to push her below the standard of excellence.

I remember Gina being in desperate need for a change in her finances. She prayed that God would bless her with increase through a new job. After God blessed her, she was initially happy and did not mind going the extra mile. However, once she settled in and became comfortable, she started taking shortcuts in her work. She would arrive daily at her exact report time, or sometimes a little late, and leave a few minutes early. Though God trusted her to be a good steward over her blessing, she took the opportunity for granted.

Gina knowingly left work undone and frequently asked for extensions to complete work for which she had previously been given ample time. Her public display of job apathy came from being passed over for a promotion and engaging in constant bickering with her supervisor. Her bitterness led her to submit incomplete assignments leaving her teammates to pick up the pieces. Gina refused take the extra step to review her completed work, opting to hurriedly glaze over assigned tasks. She would also spend excessive time surfing the Internet and taking care of personal business while on the job.

By the end of the day, Gina probably only spent two solid hours actually working, but because no one was standing over her shoulder, she chose to take advantage of her worklife freedom. The very job for which Gina prayed was eventually lost because she did not maintain what God commands of us with his standard of distinction, which far exceeds the expectations of man.

God has given you a path that was chosen based on His will for your life. Thus, all that is done by the work of your hand must be executed with excellence. Mediocrity is intolerable when you are a child of the most high. Because you are an earthly representation of Him, it is your duty to set the standard for quality work performance. One cannot represent the kingdom in a less than stellar fashion.

So, you may hate your job, feel uninspired, lack motivation, or wish that you could be at a different place in your career. Until your assignment in that place is complete, attend to each task mightily. Placing all of your effort into what you are paid to do will be pleasing unto God, for He has blessed you with the opportunity to work. While in this place, the word instructs you to appreciate your encounters with work since the experience cannot be taken to the grave. Once you are delivered or promoted from this level of vocation, you will have refined the tools needed for God's next assignment for your life. All experiences have purpose, and in order to reach maximum potential, God favors the hand of those who labor diligently.

Pray this prayer when you feel unproductive in your workspace:

> *Lord God, stir up the power of my hands. Let them not be found resting when I should be working. Let them not be found shuffling tasks rather than completing them. I ask that you remind me each time I falter that you are depending on my work to be fruitful. Lord, I want you to be proud of me for working steadily, for there is great reward in the end. Thank you in advance for stabilizing my mind so that I may do the work that is required of me. Help me to follow the lead of those that have charge over me and humble my spirit to take action even when I am no longer enthusiastic about the task. Renew my mind, Lord, and give me fresh eyes with which to view my workload. When all else fails, Lord, help me to remember that it matters how I walk through each area of my life. Grant me diligence, persistence, perseverance and the intuitiveness to complete each assignment with gumption. I ask these things in your mighty name. Amen.*

1. **Recall a time (or two) where you may have squandered your day at work. How did you overcome the unproductivity and begin to put your best foot forward? What are some strategies that you might use to remain productive at work?**

2. **Answer the above questions in the *Reflection Section.***

Walking it Out

"You shall walk in all the ways which the LORD your God has commanded you, that you may live and that it may be *well with you, and* that *you may prolong* your *days in the land which you shall possess."*
(Deut. 5.33)

Walking it out simply refers to graciously embracing life's daily offerings while simultaneously following God's directives. When life throws a curveball, walk it out. When it's pouring down blessings in your life, still walk it out. There are no shortcuts through life. You must experience all that it has to give – painful, joyous, or absolutely hideous, you have to experience it all.

Picture a mild rainstorm, if you will. Wind whistles outside your window, tearing away weak tree limbs. Lightning flashes in succession, each time illuminating the sky with more intensity. Water splatters against your windows reminding you that it will be there for a while. After the storm finally subsides, you walk outside to witness fallen shrubs, broken branches, and a pile of leaves washed up in your yard or near the drainage systems. Though this is a small inconvenience, you discard the fallen branches, rake up the leaves and move on. Like the rainstorm, we all have debris in our life that we either step over, push to the side, or clean up. Though it may sidetrack us momentarily, we must keep moving. The key to movement is to take God with you. You will find your life enriched with the full blessings of the Lord.

Challenge yourself to 'walking it out' in your worklife. Your career will be filled with moments of joy and excitement, like when you first get the new job! You will also experience frustration, similar to learning new processes and procedures for a job that is initially foreign to you. Undoubtedly, you will also experience lows such as being picked on, being overlooked, or failing at achieving a company goal. During each of these times, God is depending on you to walk in His way and be a gleaming example of how to maintain a spirit of humbleness through each phase of your career journey. You never know who is watching, so strut your best walk each day!

Pray this prayer when you have trouble "walking out" your worklife:

Heavenly Father, help me to embrace all that life has to offer with open arms. I understand that each season experienced may not feel comfortable, and there are others that may feel great. Either way, Lord, help me to continuously walk in the light of your presence as we travel this road together. When the sun is shining, place upon me a yearning to celebrate your goodness in my life. When the clouds fall, remind me that this is just a rendering of life's experiences. Nothing that I go through at work is a surprise to you. I thank you in advance for the endurance to finish the race with class and grace, not mumbling or grimacing when things don't go my way or becoming overzealous and boastful when things are awesome in my life. I praise your name and lift you up. Amen.

1. **How can you help another co-worker this week to walk through their difficulty or celebrate their accomplishments at work?**

2. **You guessed it! Write it down in the *Reflection Section.***

Enjoying the Journey

"My brethren, count it all joy when you fall into various trials, knowing that the testing of your faith produces patience. But let patience have its *perfect work, that you may be perfect and complete, lacking nothing."*
(Jas. 1.2-4)

Worklife sometimes has the potential to put a damper on parts of your day. Before you head out of the door for your 45-minute commute to work, you decide to check your email. In the first work email of the morning, your supervisor makes sure you know that the email you sent to staff was missing a few key points, and now she insists that your emails are sent to her before sending them out to the rest of the team. This is the perfect time for your mind to spiral out of control thinking about how much you hate being micromanaged. After all, why be in the role of manager, if your supervisor won't let you manage?

To make matters worse, you arrive to your job where fellow employees are gossiping in the hallway, an emergency three-hour meeting is called by the company chief, yet you still have tons of work to complete, and to top it off, you are still expected to meet specific deadlines that are just one centimeter from being unreasonable! You huff and puff thinking to yourself, "Didn't we just have a meeting yesterday? What on earth could we possibly have to talk about today?"

Each day, you grow tired of the mundane and restless with the highlighting of minor faults. Through it all, you have to stay the course and enjoy the journey. Reveling in bitterness about the upsets of the day or dwelling in the miseries of your worklife does not help you live at the peak of greatness. In order to live a life of abundant overflow, you must welcome each day as it comes. Whether it's difficult, demanding, joyous or peaceful, facing each day with an open heart helps you to process all the lessons that God has for you.

Actively seeking each day's offerings yields opportunities for development in ways you could never dream. Asking God for his divine daily intervention will help your life flourish and expose you to a keen spiritual awareness that supersedes what you would be able to observe with the natural eye. Resolve to relish each moment given and have patience with the process of life. Know that the *process* brings about *promotion*, *elevation*, and *progression*. Trust God's plan and allow him to do a major thing in your life.

Pray this prayer when you need help enjoying the worklife journey:

Lord, I come before you honoring your holy name. In this moment as I pray, impart peace over my life through each part of my career journey. I ask that each day, I seek to be empowered by possibility and enlightened with fresh thoughts about the positive aspects of life. When things are going well, Lord, I acknowledge the power of your presence. When things deteriorate in my life, Lord, I still acknowledge the power of your presence. Help me to call on you through circumstances great and small, so that your hand will bless my path. Each day I am given the opportunity to choose how I will react to what stands before me. Lead me to choose calmness, patience and joy. Grant me serenity through it all. Engulf my mind and fill my spirit with goodness and gratitude so that I may share it with others on this road that I travel. I forever praise your name, Lord. Amen.

1. **Regardless of unforeseen obstacles, how will you strive to enjoy your worklife journey today? What specific actions will you take to enjoy the day (i.e. create a new ritual, incorporate a new positive habit, etc.)?**

2. **Use the *Reflection Section* to express your new insights.**

Promoting Positivity

"And do not be conformed to this world, but be transformed by the renewing of your mind, that you may prove what is *that good and acceptable and perfect will of God."*
(Rom. 12.2)

When you are a follower of Christ, you must think of yourself as a walking billboard – an advertisement that catches the eye of all who pass your way. What do you want people to think and say when they see you? Do they stop and look, observing all of the originality it must have taken to create you? Consider these questions when you interact with colleagues. Being a child of God is a full-time job. No need to apply if you aren't up for the challenge. You thought you had work, but being pleasing to God is your top priority. In all that you do, do it to satisfy Him. All that you expect to receive at work, you must give out through your work. One mustn't selfishly hover over their gifts and expect gifts to be given.

Promote the goodness of God when you walk, talk and think. Converse with coworkers in a tone that commands respect, while simultaneously resting in your own quiet authority. Exude the qualities that you want your peers to see. Emit radiance and shower workmates with the passion that you have for your career. Your life should be an experience for all you encounter. Impart wisdom to those around you, speak to those who are consistently overlooked, and purposely practice good deeds even when you know that they may go unnoticed. Choose to divert attention away from the negative. Positivity is an action word. What will you do to enhance your optimism?

Pray this prayer when you need help promoting positivity at work:

Lord, as I strive to be more like you, shine light on the areas of my life where I can bolster my positivity. Help me to understand that I must first be the example for any behavior that I would like to receive while in my career. Work within me to foster the qualities and characteristics needed to achieve the task of radiating light, power, and love. Daily, remind me that I am a reflection of you. Therefore, I must commit to doing things the right way instead of my way. I submit to your commandment to love others as you love me. Let me not grow weary in well-doing, and let my foot not stumble as I start a new chapter of affirmation. I go confidently in the direction you would have me to with an upbeat spirit and progressive mindset. Let your presence abide within me always. Amen.

1. **Provide five (5) ways you can spread positivity at work this week. Be as creative as possible without considering any significant monetary contributions. Challenge yourself to create memories that cost nothing or very little.**

2. **List your ideas in the *Reflection Section.***

Spirit of Thanksgiving

"Enter into His gates with thanksgiving,
And *into His courts with praise. Be*
thankful to Him, and *bless His name."*
(Ps. 1.4)

Hallelujah to the most high God! He has brought you out of darkness and into the light. Sometimes, it's hard to be thankful when our lives don't go as planned. The funny part is just that, it's *our* plan and not God's divine order. When you release your life to Him, it is His will that must be done, not your own. Amazingly once you let go, God takes the reigns and creates a marvelous rendition of life – one that you could never even imagine. He is the ultimate artist. The maker of Picasso, Van Gogh, da Vinci, Michelangelo, Kahlo, and Rembrandt, God is the supreme giver of gifts and talents. You are a masterpiece in your own right. Give yourself fully over to the master creator and be thankful that He can do a great work in you just as he has done in others.

As you master your work this week, do it with gladness and thanksgiving. Consider how you prayed for the job in the first place, or how you were without a job for a period of time. You may have had to file for unemployment or borrow money from friends and family to get you over the financial mountain that seemed so impossible to scale. However, you kept the faith that God would bring you through. You made sure that you kept looking for that perfect job, showing up for interview after interview until His promise to increase you came to pass.

Thank the Lord for shining his face upon you even when you did not deserve such favor. When God smiles upon you, remember that you are free to dance in the rain and bask in the sunshine simply because you are His child. Praise Him for the rest of your days for He is worthy to be praised!

Pray this prayer of thanksgiving for how he has increased you through gainful employment:

Lord, I thank you simply for being who you are. I exalt you for your awesome power. Thank you for being my protector, my sword and shield. While at work, you encamp me daily and grant mercy without me asking. I bless your name and lift you up on high! You are so worthy to be praised. Thank you for sending your only begotten son down to save me from myself! I am excited because I live in you and you live in me. Because I carry you with me, I can immediately find joy and peace. Oh Lord, I praise you so that I can be a beacon of light and minister to those around me with the power you have given. I will tell all of your good works through my actions and deeds. Let me not forget that I have victory in life because of your unfailing hand. Thank you for lifting me in my areas of weakness so that I may not stumble. Thank you for each gift and desire that you have placed within me and for the effective use of my talent while at work. As I move throughout the day, I will be sure to give your name glory for all of the great things you have done. I lift my hands in adoration and worship you. Thank you, God. Amen.

1. **Think about your past week at work. What has occurred that makes you thankful?**

2. **Record your thoughts in the *Reflection Section.***

You Made It!

Congratulations on making it through this 21-day devotional! Now that you have committed to having daily-dedicated time with God, don't stop! Continue your relationship with Him by writing your own prayers and thoughts to God each day. You can even reread this devotional to continue edifying your spirit.

I wanted to create a resource for women who were experiencing difficulty in the workplace. My hope is that this text has served its purpose for your needs. Since completing the devotional, you should feel closer to God, confident in walking through workplace difficulty, have a sense of peace, and have a desire to further develop your relationship with Him. If you still need support in your worklife journey, feel free to go back and reread the sections that were most meaningful to you. Remember that you are not alone on this journey. This is not your final destination. As you travel down your predestined path, allow God to help you navigate the next sea you must sail. Stay in peace and trust Him. His outcome will yield greater than you have ever imagined!

SECTION II PART I

Reflection Section

Introspection is good for the soul.
Self-assessment never gets old.
Answer the questions as they have been asked.
Commit each day to this cleansing task.

Devotional Title: *When you are Worried*
Corresponding Activity: What is your specific workplace worry? What will help you give it to God?

Devotional Title: *When you are Under Attack*
Corresponding Activity: You may come under attack at work for many reasons that may not be immediately revealed. Think of a time you may have experienced personal attack. Write about how you plan to or have already overcome workplace attacks.

Devotional Title: *Colliding with Naysayers*
Corresponding Activity: If you have not already done so, consider the friend(s) on whom you can depend to stand with you in times of collision. How can you nurture those relationships and keep them strong?

Devotional Title: *When you feel Defeated*
Corresponding Activity: When things don't go the way we expect, we are often caught off guard, and it can take a while to regain ourselves. Reflect on how you can overcome feelings of defeat while at work.

Devotional Title: *Perfectly Imperfect*
Corresponding Activity: Reflect on how you have recovered from a mistake you made at work. What steps did you take to rectify the mistake? How did God show up to guide you through the situation?

Devotional Title: *Feeling Undervalued and Unappreciated*
Corresponding Activity: Reflect on how God validates you each day. How has His goodness towards you made you feel both valued and appreciated?

Devotional Title: *Getting Unstuck*
Corresponding Activity: How will you choose to get unstuck? List three (3) actionable steps to get you on the road to clarity.

Devotional Title: *Finding Hope through Hurt*
Corresponding Activity: What *hurt* have you had to overcome in order to be *hopeful* about your worklife? What growth have you seen within yourself as a result of getting past the pain?

Devotional Title: *I am Not Alone*
Corresponding Activity: What other techniques might you use when feeling alone at work that also support your relationship with God?

Devotional Title: *Finding Peace*
Corresponding Activity: Challenge: Create your own prayer for peace. What do you want to request of God?

Devotional Title: *Walking in the Light of God*
Corresponding Activity: What else might you add to the outlined prayer to cover your need to walk in the light of God? (See corresponding prayer in Section I, Part III)

Devotional Title: *God Is Where the Good Stuff Is*
Corresponding Activity: Challenge: Consider all the blessings God has provided in your life. List the most recent worklife blessing that surely could not have been achieved without the help of the Lord.

Devotional Title: *From Fear to Faith*
Corresponding Activity: What are some ways that you can overcome fear at work?

Devotional Title: *Turning the Other Cheek*
Corresponding Activity: In the flesh, going tit-for-tat with your adversary may be gratifying, but this is a fleeting moment. What instances have you had to practice what God said and turn the other cheek? How did the situation ultimately resolve?

Devotional Title: *Pray your Way*
Corresponding Activity: Challenge: Write your best prayer to God. Have it to encompass each obstacle you are currently facing at work. Talk to Him about everything that troubles you. After completion, leave it in God's hands and continuously proclaim the victory over your trials.

Devotional Title: *Practicing the Fruits*
Corresponding Activity: Which fruit do you have the most trouble practicing at work? What actions will you actively commit to so that the troublesome fruit can be made stronger in your life?

Devotional Title: *Being Productive*
Corresponding Activity: Recall a time (or two) where you may have squandered your day at work. How did you overcome the unproductivity and begin to put your best foot forward? What are some strategies that you might use to remain productive at work?

Devotional Title: *Walking it Out*
Corresponding Activity: How can you help another co-worker this week to walk through their difficulty or celebrate their accomplishments at work?

Devotional Title: *Enjoying the Journey*
Corresponding Activity: Regardless of unforeseen obstacles, how will you strive to enjoy your worklife journey today? What specific actions will you take to enjoy the day (i.e. create a new ritual, incorporate a new positive habit, etc.)?

Devotional Title: *Promoting Positivity*
Corresponding Activity: Provide five (5) ways you can spread positivity at work this week. Be as creative as possible without considering any significant monetary contributions. Challenge yourself to create memories that cost nothing or very little.

Devotional Title: *Spirit of Thanksgiving*
Corresponding Activity: Think about your past week at work. What has occurred that makes you thankful?

SECTION II PART II

WORK HAG WORRY

If your workplace is not sound, do
commit to writing it down.
Events will soon be lost in flight
if at first you do not write.
Give full description, names, dates and times.
All in one place, your notes you shall find.

How to Use this Section

During my journey, I found it helpful to keep an account of all interactions with my work hag so that I could use it to tell my story to the proper workplace authorities if and when the time came to plead my case of workplace bullying and harassment.

As you complete the *Work Hag Worry Section*, be mindful of my personally crafted definition of workplace bullying and a work hag. Knowing how to identify the two lends validation to your experience. Use this section to record specific details of what happens on the job in relation to your work hag. This will be a useful tool should you have to take additional steps of action in the process of overcoming workplace bullying.

Workplace Bullying | verb: The repeated display of psychological and emotional violence exhibited by co-workers and/or supervisors against a person(s) causing intimidation, fear, anguish, humiliation, despair, ostracism and undue stress.

Work Hag | noun: Maliciously vicious employees whose primary goal is to void the workplace of positive human interaction and use their venomous nature to poison the climate and culture of work communities.

When recording your encounters, remember the importance of keeping all notes very detailed and up-to-date. Instances of bullying, discrimination and intimidation will require solid evidence. The following chart will be a helpful resource if you need to recall information should your situation escalate to reporting offenses.

Write incidents down shortly after they occur and within the same day so that all details are accurate. The longer you wait to record information, the less clear and precise the details become. Stay away from writing down assumptions or drawing conclusions. Tell the story from beginning to end, and stick to facts when recounting events with your work hag(s).

Date & Time of Occurrence:	***Location:*** *(Example: 2nd floor near rm. 102)*	***People Involved:***
Notes: (Facts only)		

Date & Time of Occurrence:	***Location:*** *(Example: 2nd floor near rm. 102)*	***People Involved:***
Notes: (Facts only)		

Date & Time of Occurrence:	*Location:* *(Example: 2nd floor near rm. 102)*	*People Involved:*

Notes: (Facts only)

Date & Time of Occurrence:	***Location:*** *(Example: 2nd floor near rm. 102)*	***People Involved:***
Notes: (Facts only)		

Date & Time of Occurrence:	***Location:*** *(Example: 2nd floor near rm. 102)*	***People Involved:***

Notes: (Facts only)

Date & Time of Occurrence:	***Location:*** *(Example: 2nd floor near rm. 102)*	***People Involved:***

Notes: (Facts only)

Date & Time of Occurrence:	***Location:*** ***(Example: 2nd floor near rm. 102)***	***People Involved:***
Notes: (Facts only)		

Date & Time of Occurrence:	***Location:*** *(Example: 2nd floor near rm. 102)*	***People Involved:***
Notes: (Facts only)		

Date & Time of Occurrence:	***Location:*** ***(Example: 2nd floor near rm. 102)***	***People Involved:***
Notes: (Facts only)		

Date & Time of Occurrence:	***Location:*** *(Example: 2nd floor near rm. 102)*	***People Involved:***
Notes: (Facts only)		

Date & Time of Occurrence:	***Location:*** ***(Example: 2nd floor near rm. 102)***	***People Involved:***
Notes: (Facts only)		

Date & Time of Occurrence:	***Location:*** *(Example: 2nd floor near rm. 102)*	***People Involved:***
Notes: (Facts only)		

Date & Time of Occurrence:	*Location:* *(Example: 2nd floor near rm. 102)*	*People Involved:*
Notes: (Facts only)		

Date & Time of Occurrence:	*Location:* *(Example: 2nd floor near rm. 102)*	*People Involved:*
Notes: (Facts only)		

Date & Time of Occurrence:	***Location:*** *(Example: 2nd floor near rm. 102)*	***People Involved:***

Notes: (Facts only)

Date & Time of Occurrence:	***Location:*** *(Example: 2nd floor near rm. 102)*	***People Involved:***
Notes: (Facts only)		

Date & Time of Occurrence:	***Location:*** *(Example: 2nd floor near rm. 102)*	***People Involved:***
Notes: (Facts only)		

Date & Time of Occurrence:	***Location:*** *(Example: 2nd floor near rm. 102)*	***People Involved:***

Notes: (Facts only)

Date & Time of Occurrence:	***Location:*** ***(Example: 2nd floor near rm. 102)***	***People Involved:***
Notes: (Facts only)		

Date & Time of Occurrence:	***Location:*** *(Example: 2nd floor near rm. 102)*	***People Involved:***
Notes: (Facts only)		

Date & Time of Occurrence:	***Location:*** *(Example: 2nd floor near rm. 102)*	***People Involved:***
Notes: (Facts only)		

Biblical References

Part I:

When you are Worried

"Be anxious for nothing, but in everything by prayer and supplication, with thanksgiving, let your requests be made known unto God; and the peace of God, which surpasses all understanding, will guard your hearts and minds thorough Christ Jesus."
(Phil. 4.6, 7)

When you are Under Attack

"Though I walk in the midst of trouble,
you will revive me;You will stretch out
Your hand against the wrath of my enemies,
andYour right hand will save me."
(Ps. 138.7)

Colliding with Naysayers

"A fool's mouth is *his destruction, and his lips* are *the snare of his soul."* (Prov. 18.7)

When you feel Defeated

"Finally, my brethren, be strong in the Lord and in the power of His might. Put on the whole armor of God, that you may be able to stand against the wiles of the devil. For we do not wrestle against flesh and blood, but against principalities, against powers, against the rulers of the darkness of this age, against spiritual hosts of wickedness in the heavenly places. Therefore take up the whole armor of God, that you may be able to withstand in the evil day, and having done all, to stand." (Eph. 6.10-13)

Part II:

Perfectly Imperfect

"For we all stumble in many things. If anyone does not stumble in word, he is *a perfect man, able also to bridle the whole body."* (Jas. 3.2)

Feeling Undervalued and Unappreciated

"You were bought at a price; do not become slaves of men." (1 Cor. 7.23)

Getting Unstuck

"... but we also glory in tribulations, knowing that tribulation produces perseverance; and perseverance, character; and character, hope."
(Rom. 5.3, 4)

Finding Hope through Hurt

"Be of good courage, And He shall strengthen your heart, All you who hope in the Lord."
(Ps. 31.24)

Part III:

I am not Alone

"And the Lord, He is the One who goes before you. He will be with you, He will not leave you nor forsake you; do not fear nor be dismayed."
(Deut. 31.8)

Finding Peace

"Peace I leave with you, My peace I give to you; not as the world gives do I give to you. Let not your heart be troubled, neither let it be afraid."
(John 14.27, 28)

"These things I have spoken to you, that in Me you may have peace. In the world you will have tribulation; but be of good cheer, I have overcome the world."
(John 16.33)

Walking in the Light of God

*"Let your light so shine before men,
that they may see your good works and
glorify your Father in heaven."*
(Matt. 5.16)

God Is Where the Good Stuff Is

*"Finally, brethren, whatever things are true,
whatever things* are *noble, whatever things* are
just, whatever things are *pure, whatever things*
are *lovely, whatever things* are *of good report,
if* there is *any virtue and if* there is *anything
praiseworthy – meditate on these things."*
(Phil. 4.8)

Part IV:

From Fear to Faith

*"He who dwells in the secret place of the Most High
Shall abide under the shadow of the Almighty.
I will say of the Lord, 'He is my refuge and my
fortress; My God, in Him I will Trust.' Surely He
shall deliver you from the snare of the fowler and
from the perilous pestilence. He shall cover you
with His feathers, and under His wings you shall
take refuge; His truth shall be your shield and
buckler.You shall not be afraid of the terror by
night, nor of the arrow that flies by day, nor of*

the pestilence that walks in darkness, nor of the destruction that lays waste at noonday. A thousand may fall at your side, and ten thousand at your right hand; But it shall not come near you."
(Ps. 91.1-7)

Turning the Other Cheek

"But I say to you who hear: Love your enemies, do good to those who hate you, bless those who curse you, and pray for those who spitefully use you. To him who strikes you on the one cheek, offer the other also. And from him who takes away your cloak, do not withhold your tunic either."
(Luke 6.27-29)

Pray Your Way

"Now this is the confidence that we have in Him, that if we ask anything according to His will, He hears us. And if we know that He hears us, whatever we ask, we know that we have the petitions that we have asked of Him."
(1 John 5.14, 15)

Practicing the Fruits

"But the fruit of the Spirit is love, joy, peace, longsuffering, kindness, goodness, faithfulness, gentleness, self-control. Against such there is no law."
(Gal. 5.22, 23)

Part V:

Being Productive

"Whatever your hand finds to do, do it *with your might; for there* is *no work or device or knowledge or wisdom in the grave where you are going."*
(Eccles. 9.10)

"He who is slothful in his work is a brother to him who is a great destroyer."
(Prov. 18.9)

Walking it Out

"You shall walk in all the ways which the LORD your God has commanded you, that you may live and that it may be *well with you, and* that *you may prolong* your *days in the land which you shall possess."*
(Deut. 5.33)

Enjoying the Journey

"My brethren, count it all joy when you fall into various trials, knowing that the testing of your faith produces patience. But let patience have its *perfect work, that you may be perfect and complete, lacking nothing."*
(Jas 1.2-4)

Promoting Positivity

"And do not be conformed to this world,
but be transformed by the renewing of your
mind, that you may prove what is *that good*
and acceptable and perfect will of God."
(ROM. 12.2)

Spirit of Thanksgiving

"Enter into His gates with thanksgiving,
And *into His courts with praise. Be*
thankful to Him, and *bless His name."*
(PS. 100.4)

For more information on *The Daniel Fast:*

1. Read the book of Daniel
2. Read *The Daniel Fast*

Gregory, Susan. 2010. *The Daniel Fast.* Grand Rapids, MI: Tyndale House Publishers, Inc.

1. Visit the Website: www.daniel-fast.com

About the Author
A Touch of Tiffany

Hi, Transformer! My name is Tiffany A. Washington, a motivational speaker, author, and success coach who helps frustrated career women like you stop hating your job so that you can live a life you truly love! This mission is achieved through workshops, online and live trainings, private and group coaching, and digital products. I am also the creator of the motivational and worklife YouTube series, *Two Minutes with Tiffany* and *Women at Work*.

My desire to help others succeed in their work and personal lives sprung out of my struggle with workplace bullying and female team dysfunction. Though it may seem a little cliché, I am a living testimony of how your mess can really turn into your MESSage. Thankfully, I have used these unique experiences to inspire other women who grapple with similar issues on the job or just simply hate their place of employment for a myriad of reasons!

Thank you for joining me on this journey towards more joy and fulfillment in your work and personal life. I look forward to bringing you targeted content that will help you find your fashion (the way in which you uniquely convey yourself to the world), and revive your passion (renew the excellence within and follow your God-given goals/dreams/aspirations).

Always,

Tiffany A. Washington
Founder and CEO | Tranformation7

Transformation 7 by Tiffany A. Washington

Transformation7 by Tiffany A. Washington is designed with you in mind! Consider the life of a caterpillar. This creature starts out crawling…slowly…to each destination, unable to fully protect itself from predators because of its sluggish movement. Though it has many legs, it gets nowhere fast. However, the beauty in the caterpillar is not truly realized until it undergoes the delicate metamorphosis process. Encased in a cocoon, its body experiences a complete transformation. Once the process is complete, a gorgeous butterfly emerges! It is now capable of flying to each destination, and onlookers are awestruck by its amazing beauty!

Just like the butterfly, we all have our moments of moving slowly through life feeling unprotected from the storms that life brews. Yet as we continue to live, our circumstances morph us into beautifully resilient human beings who serve as blessings to others who engage in our presence.

The number seven (7) represents completion. It is the favorite number of many (including me) for this very reason! Seven marks the end. Think of this number as a symbol of old things passed away in your life and the start of something great! Your current situation is not your final destination. Transition your thoughts towards the transformation of your life into a body of work to be admired. Live the life that makes you feel free and happy. You are strong. You are courageous. You are bold. You are a Transformer! Go forth and conquer all that you desire with zeal and passion.

How to Contact Tiffany A. Washington

To find out more about Transformation7 by Tiffany A. Washington and our products and coaching services, visit our website at www.transformation7.com and on the following social media platforms:

Facebook: www.facebook.com/T7byTiffany/
Twitter: https://twitter.com/T7byTiffany
Instagram: www.instagram.com/Transformation7/
Periscope: www.pscp.tv/Transformation7/
YouTube: goo.gl/Rg8aLI
(Transformation7 by Tiffany A. Washington)

For more information on our individual and group coaching packages, as well as speaking engagement availability, please contact coachme@transformation7.com.

To book Tiffany for professional speaking engagements, please submit your inquiry to tiffany@transformation7.com or contact us at www.transformation7.com//speaking-engagements/.